THE SADBOOK COLLECTIONS

I

adventures of a stick figure human

s a r a   b a r k a t

ts T. S. Poetry Press • New York

T. S. Poetry Press
New York

Tspoetry.com

ISBN 978-1-943120-71-0

Barkat, Sara
    [Comics.]
    The Sadbook Collections 1: adventures of a
    stick figure human
    ISBN 978-1-943120-71-0

visit **sadbook.substack.com** to sign up for the (mostly) daily comic The Sadbook Collections!

Do you see something in this collection that you'd like to order as a print? Just ask the Artist to add it to the Sadbook shop!

Ask on Instagram at **instagram.com/sadbookcollections**

or on Substack at **sadbook.substack.com**

TABLE OF CONTENTS

FROM THE ARTIST

why sadbook, why art

If you can draw a straight line and a circle, you can draw a stick figure. The "form" of a stick figure is simple, but what makes a stick figure *human*? For that, your stick figure needs character. Needs moods and quirks and particularities, needs dynamism—a gesture drawing pared down to the essentials.

Art is frequently pretentious. This isn't Art's fault, not really. Anything that collects expertise brings that along with it, like talent's evil twin. There are very many people who claim "I can't draw," and what they really mean is "I am not an artist." This may be true. But drawing itself isn't difficult. It can be as simple as a few sticks and a circle. What stops people from drawing is not usually technical skill, but an inability to *imagine* onto a page. "I can't *do* that." "I'm not *that* person." "I'm no *good* at it." Even artists get this way! Even Sadbook's artist gets this way, sometimes. She looks at all her favorite artists and sighs, "I'll never be able to do *that*."

When the Artist first created the concept that would become Sadbook, it's true that she was thinking about none of these things. She was mostly thinking that she was sad, and that she wanted a small person to inhabit the untangleable feeling. But once the "Sad Book" was drawn, the Artist realized that this was not the end of the story. A stick figure with so many existential thoughts might become something more.

Sometimes all the things you can't do stack up and up and *up*, until you're so afraid of starting anything at all because you might—*gasp*—do it badly! Or maybe there are other reasons that you stall, like feeling sad and a little in need of a stick figure, when the big, dramatic, impressive art isn't going to arrive.

But that's okay. When it comes down to it, Art is about spirit, about communicating. And *visual art* is about communicating what can't be said in words.

—Sara Barkat, illustrator of *The Sadbook Collections* comic
and *The Yellow Wall-Paper: A Graphic Novel* ; author of
The Shivering Ground & Other Stories

THE SADBOOK COLLECTIONS

NEW COMIC

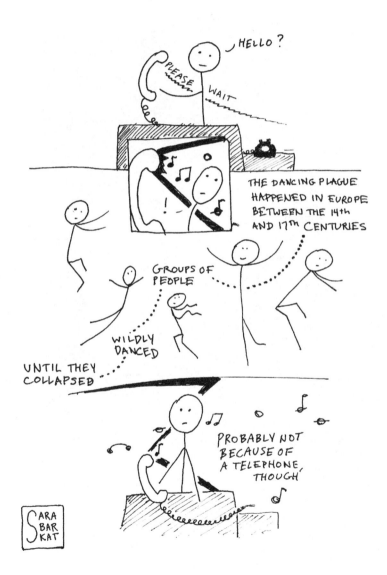

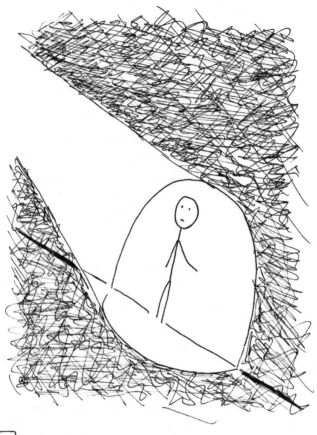

SEEN.

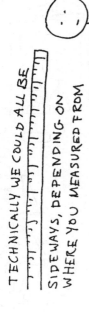

TECHNICALLY WE COULD ALL BE
SIDEWAYS, DEPENDING ON
WHERE YOU MEASURED FROM

IF I GET A NEW MATTRESS, WILL I
SLEEP BETTER?

MIRROR

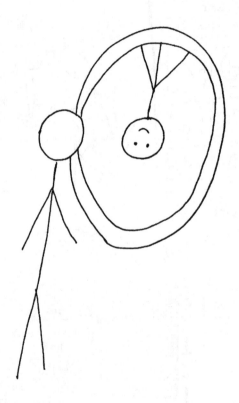

FILMING

SIGN UP

please enter your email

HUMAN@SADBOOKCOLLECTIONS.COM

ENTER

THANK YOU! NOW, WE JUST NEED A FEW MORE DETAILS
BEFORE WE CAN CREATE YOUR NEW ACCOUNT

phone number * _____

government photo ID * [UPLOAD]

first born child * ☐ I agree to the following

click. click. click.

GREAT!
YOU'RE ALL SET!
WELCOME TO
SOCIAL MEDIA!

LIGHT SWITCH

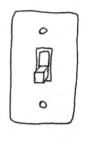 VS

Flick!

1 STEP

A) FLICK

3 STEPS

A) STOP
B) LOOK
C) SLAM

I DON'T LIKE THESE NEW LIGHT SWITCHES...

(also, they are ugly)

REMASTER

 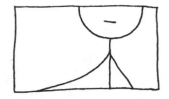

HMM...

STORM

I'VE MADE SOME PRETTY FANCY ART STUFF...

BUT RECENTLY, WHEN I TRY TO DRAW...

THE TRUTH IS, WHAT I LIKE TO DO MOST IS JUST...

DOODLE.

QUILTING

YOU CAN SEW AS MANY
SQUARES AS YOU LIKE

BUT AS LONG AS YOU
DON'T KNOW HOW TO
PUT THEM TOGETHER

... ALL YOU HAVE ARE SCRAPS.

TWO TO A BED

BAT !

SWIVEL
SWIVEL

YOU NEED HEALTH INSURANCE

but i'm not sick...

THAT OLD STORY...

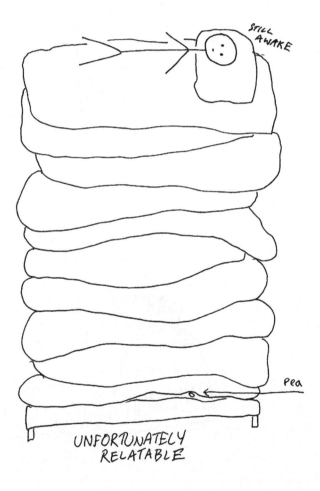

WORD SEARCH

FISHING

IN THE ZOO,
THE ANIMALS
LOOK AT YOU

DANCING

PIRATE MY WORK

(JUST KEEP THE FLAG)
ON IT, OKAY?

CREATIVE WRITING

WAITING FOR SNOW

... NONE CAME

VISIT

COMFY

ALMOST EMPTY JAR

PRINTING

INTERVIEW WITH A STICK FIGURE

— SO, WHERE DO YOU SEE
YOURSELF IN FIVE YEARS?

...

ON A PIECE
OF PAPER!

...

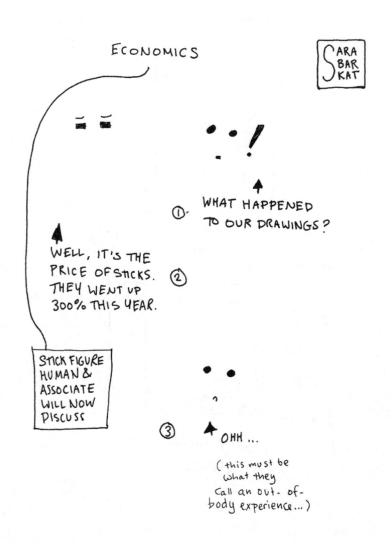

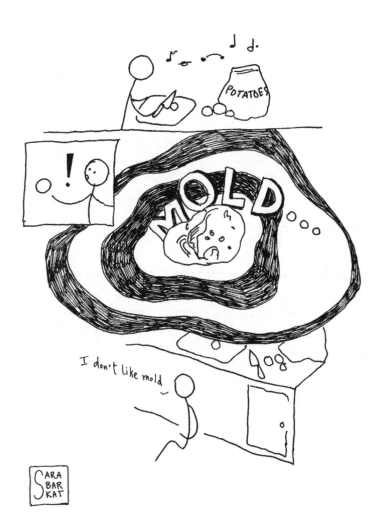

IN EXILE

BIG KNIFE

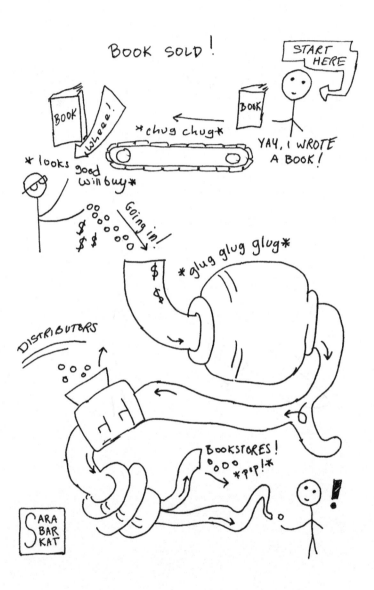

AIRPORT SECURITY

SOMETIMES A HUMAN

INJURY

O NO!
I'M BLEEDING!

SICK & TIRED

blankie

MAKING PLANS

S ARA BAR KAT

I AM SO EXCITED TO GO TO THE AQUARIUM! IT DOESN'T CLOSE TILL 5 SO I WILL BE ABLE TO LOOK AT FISH AND SEAHORSES AND TINY TINY JELLYFISH!

HELLO! ARE YOU FEELING LIKE GOING TO THE AQUARIUM WITH ME?

YES, GOING TO THE AQUARIUM. IT SOUNDS GOOD. AND WE CAN STOP AT THE MALL ON THE WAY BACK SINCE WE WON'T BE IN THE AQUARIUM FOR THAT LONG.

OH... YES. YEAH...

NEAR DEATH EXPERIENCE

AND SO I WONDER (IN BETWEEN BEING SO SCARED)
AM I HAPPY WITH MY LIFE? HAVE I PUT
SOMETHING INTO THE WORLD THAT I'M PROUD OF?
IF I WERE NOT GOING TO WAKE UP AGAIN,
COULD I STILL KNOW THAT I'D DONE
WHAT I COULD — LEFT BEHIND A FEW
THINGS THAT SHOW WHERE I'M GOING,
WHAT I'M TRYING TO ACCOMPLISH? IF I
BECAME A TRAGIC TALE, WOULD
THERE STILL BE SOME TRIUMPH IN IT?
WILL OTHERS UNDERSTAND? CAN I
BE CONTENT?

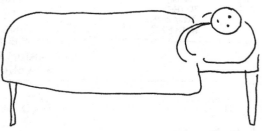

... yes. I think so.

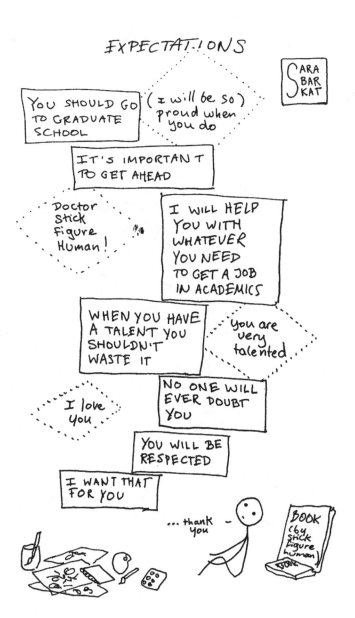

SAME FACES!

APRIL

APRIL IS THE
CRUELLEST MONTH,

BREEDING LILACS OUT OF THE DEAD LAND

SARA
BAR
KAT

— THE WASTE LAND
T. S. ELIOT

STUCK

ANEMONE

WASHING MACHINE

THE CLOTHES MUST BE HAVING FUN...

thoughtful

WE BOTH OPEN JARS!

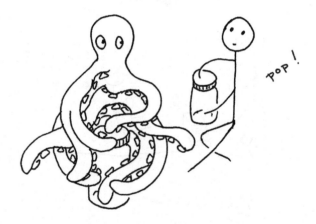

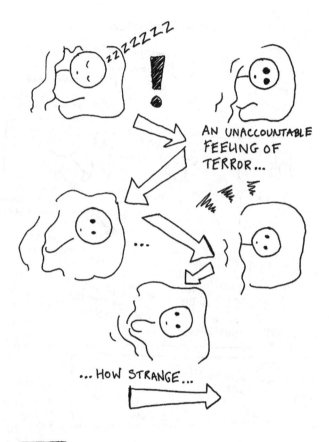

MONDAY

I AM VERY MUCH TOO TIRED TO DO ANYTHING

NUTSHELL

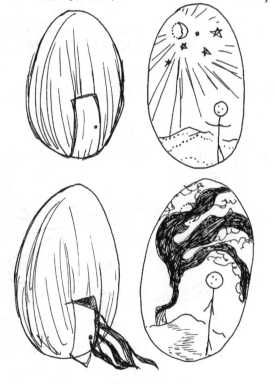

O GOD,
I COULD BE BOUNDED
IN A NUTSHELL,

AND COUNT MYSELF
A KING OF INFINITE
SPACE,

WERE IT NOT THAT I HAVE BAD DREAMS.

— HAMLET
WILLIAM
SHAKESPEARE

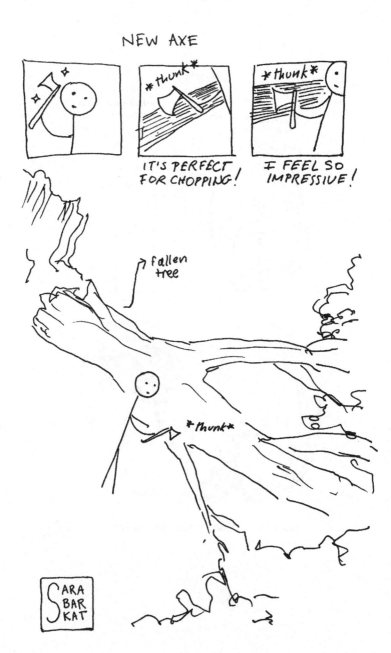

ESSENTIAL

YES, I DID SOMEHOW
END UP WITH VERY
MANY ESSENTIAL OILS...

they don't fit anywhere

BUT I NEED
ALL OF THEM!

SARA BARKAT

MUCH MADNESS IS DIVINEST SENSE
poem by emily dickinson
TO A DISCERNING EYE
SARA BAR KAT
MUCH SENSE -
THE STARKEST MADNESS
BEEP! BEEP!
BEEP!
BEEP!

KAFKA

the metamorphosis

Ceiling fan

twap
thwap

... BUT I DID NOT KNOW
HOW THE STORY WOULD LEAVE
ME WITH ████████████
██████ THE
KNOWLEDGE THAT THE WORLD IS
A SAD, MISERABLE, ████████
ABSOLUTELY POINTLESS PLACE.
I JUST THOUGHT IT WAS A STORY
OF A MAN WHO TURNED INTO A BUG!

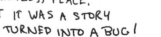

PINNED

I AM REALLY VERY TIRED

MUSIC

SWING!

The Persistence of Memory

Nighthawks

A SMALL CUP OF COFFEE

THE SCREAM

DRACULA'S CASTLE

SARA BAR KAT

WE WENT TO DRACULA'S CASTLE FOR TEA...

AND LEFT A SWEATER BEHIND.

NOW HE WON'T GIVE IT BACK...

I WONDER IF IT MAKES HIM FEEL COZY?

CHILDHOOD TROUBLES

WHEN YOU ARE A CHILD, NO ONE WILL EVER LET YOU DO *ANYTHING* BY YOURSELF.

CAN'T HANG OUT AT THE LIBRARY...

CAN'T EVEN GO IN THE TORTURE EXHIBIT....!

WHAT IS THIS WORLD COMING TO?

BEST CUP

I HAVE LOTS OF CUPS.

BUT...

ONE OF THEM IS VERY MUCH THE BEST.

I USE IT ALWAYS.

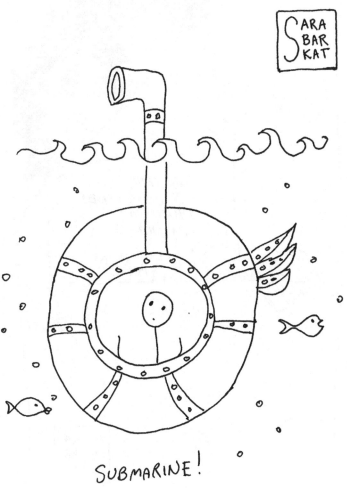

SUBMARINE!

BUTTERCUPS!
they are so shiny!

FADING AWAY

i wonder where

my body goes

when I'm not
in it

MARKETING

I DO NOT LIKE TO MARKET
VERY MUCH ...

BECAUSE ...

I WOULD RATHER PLAY
WITH SMALL ROCKS!

BATH

Splashing!
around!

CIRCADIAN

SARA BAR KAT

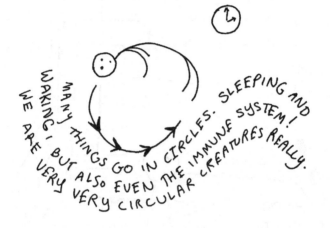

MANY THINGS GO IN CIRCLES. SLEEPING AND WAKING, BUT ALSO EVEN THE IMMUNE SYSTEM! WE ARE VERY VERY CIRCULAR CREATURES REALLY.

IN HUMANS, IMMUNE RESPONSES ARE STRONGER IN THE SECOND HALF OF THE NIGHT AND EARLY MORNING HOURS.

a circadian based inflammatory response — implications for respiratory disease and treatment (Comas, M., Gordon, C.J., Oliver, B.G., et al. Sleep Science Practice)

PUDDLE

when the water is still the reflections
of the trees are like a whole upside-down
world, and then, when the water
splashes, everything turns to diamonds
and patterns of light...!

(Also, it makes splashy noises)

BOREDOM

THIS IS A SAD DAY!
NOTHING
WHATSOEVER IS
HAPPENING!

... WHAT'S THIS?

A SMALL BIRD
HAS LANDED!

AND IT IS BEGINNING TO SING!

THE AIR QUALITY IS BAD TODAY.

KEEP THE WINDOWS SHUT!

SMOKE RISES FROM THE RIVER.

CACTUS

I HAVE A NEW CACTUS!

HE IS PRICKLY BUT CUTE!

ONCE A MONTH, I HAVE TO MIST IT WITH A SPRAY BOTTLE. THAT'S IT!

(cactuses are easy to take care of.)

(... supposedly)

* reach *

O NO! HE SNAGGED ON MY SLEEVE!

DON'T WORRY LITTLE GUY, SOON YOU WILL BE RIGHT AS RAIN.

* back in * * pat pat *

THE FOLDABLE PLANT

S ARA
  BAR
  KAT

I HAVE A FOLDABLE PLANT. IT IS SO VERY VERY INTERESTING...

EACH STEM IS CURLY AND GREEN, AND ITS LEAVES ARE

PURPLE!

DURING THE DAY IT LOOKS LIKE THIS...

AND DURING THE NIGHT...

← side view

IT FOLDS UP LIKE AN UMBRELLA!

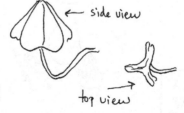

top view →

CHERRY-PICKING

BECAUSE THERE ARE
SO SO MANY OF THEM...

YOU WILL NEVER GET
THEM ALL!

GOING TO A WEDDING

I DO NOT LIKE THIS OUTFIT

OR THIS OUTFIT

OR THAT ONE EITHER...

mirror

SARA BAR KAT

THE PIT OF DESPAIR

I will never ever ever find something good to wear...

OH!

somehow, the perfect outfit

AFTER MANY TRIALS
↓
AND TERRORS
↓
AND TRIBULATIONS

NO UMBRELLA

DUCT TAPE

COPY & PASTE

I DO NOT LIKE
TO COPY & PASTE...

...133 TIMES.

SPY

TALL WAVES

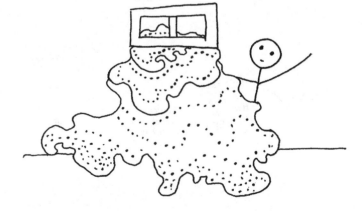

THE GREAT WAVE OFF NEW YORK

HEAVEN

SARA BAR KAT

I DREAMED THAT HEAVEN WAS A LONG ROAD

POPULATED BY PEOPLE WE DIDN'T NECESSARILY KNOW, OR LIKE, OR AGREE WITH,

AND WHO WE DIDN'T EXPECT ANY HELP FROM.

... BUT WE DID.

WE ALL HELPED EACH OTHER ALONG THAT ROAD.

BALLOON

IN BOXES

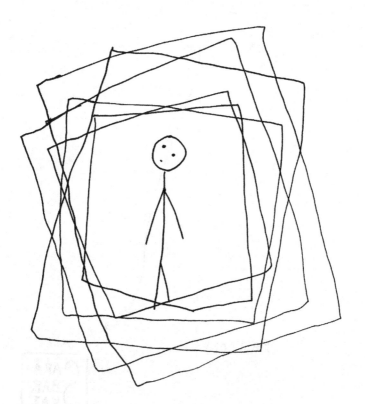

DRAW MORE

SCHEDULED

TODAY   TOMORROW   →

I REALLY NEED TO DRAW MORE PICTURES... THIS IS GETTING SERIOUS... HOW DID THIS HAPPEN? I WAS AHEAD 2 WEEKS AGO... TIME IS MY ENEMY!

ignored

CONCENTRIC

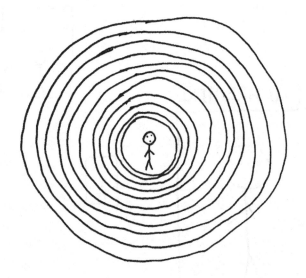

GUITAR

SUNHAT

REALLY BAD LUCK

S ARA
  BAR
  KAT

I KEEP STATS OF MY WRITING.
REALLY MOTIVATING TO SEE
"139,000 words"

→

LESS SO WHEN YOU
ACCIDENTALLY
DELETE ALL THE
STATS FOR THE
PAST HOW-MANY
MONTHS*

* not the
writing though.
Just the
wordcount #s
fortunately

ALSO, THERE IS A MOSQUITO FLYING AROUND.
PROBABLY TRYING TO EAT ME.

OK

more bad news
on the phone

MARSHMALLOW

STICKY

BUTTERFLY SHIRT

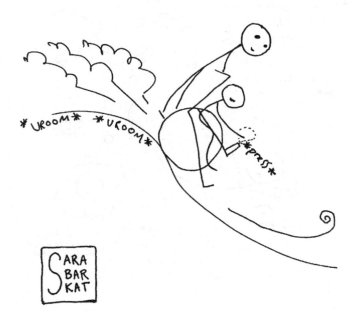

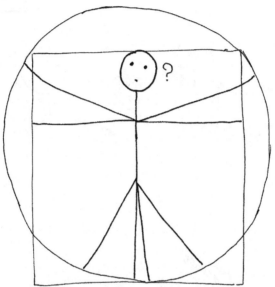

THE PROPORTIONS OF THE HUMAN STICK FIGURE
AFTER LEONARDO AFTER VITRUVIUS

The length of the outspread arms is however long it needs in order to reach the edge of the circle, or whatever is funny. From below the chin to the top of the head is circular. the maximum width of the shoulders is nothing. The foot is also nothing. the eyes and mouth are a triangle.

SPLATTER

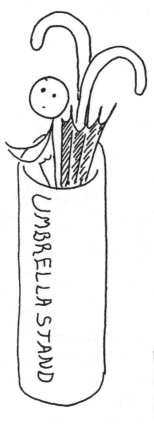

PARTY'S CONCLUSION

← need some space

AT THE END OF
THE PARTY, I AM
VERY TIRED.
BUT THESE THREE
CHAIRS ARE GOOD
TO LIE DOWN ON
FOR A MINUTE.

... IT IS SO LOUD!

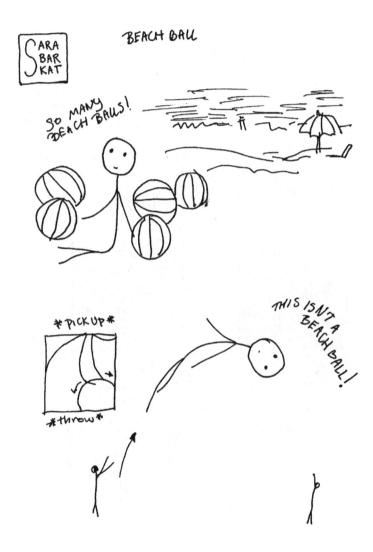

NAP

DUCKS IN A ROW

NOIR

WRITER'S BLOCK

SO MUCH SCIENCE!

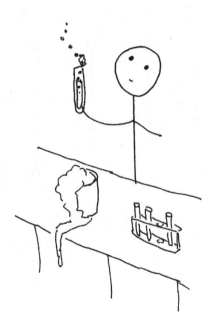

SIX FIGURES

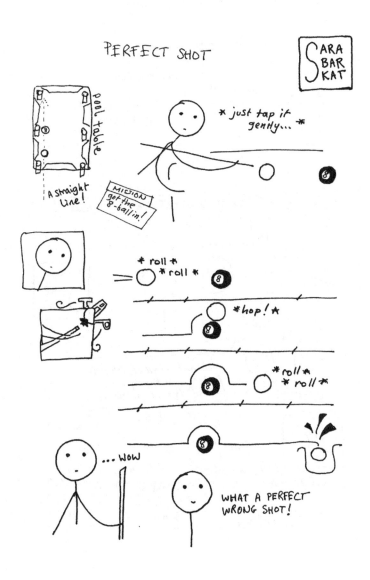

DRINKING BAR CHART

NOW & VENN DIAGRAM

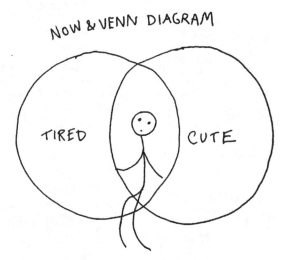

SARA BAR KAT

S'MORES CLUB

I HAVE THE GREATEST MOST WONDERFULLEST IDEA EVER... A S'MORES CLUB!

EVERY MONTH, YOU WOULD GET SOMETHING LIKE...

peanut butter & jelly
→ peanut flavored graham cracker
→ jelly flavored marshmallow
dark chocolate.

Chai
→ chocolate graham cracker
milk chocolate
→ cardamom & other chai spices flavored marshmallow

green tea & lavender
→ lavender flavored marshmallow
→ green tea white chocolate

Cider
→ graham cracker drizzled with icing
→ apple cider spices - cinnamon, nutmeg flavored marshmallow
dark chocolate with candied orange peel

...YUM

a ball of yarn

LEAF BLOWER

VROOM

VROOM VROOM

SARA BAR KAT

MAYBE SWALLOWED UP

Sara Barkat • 203

SO MANY SPIDERS

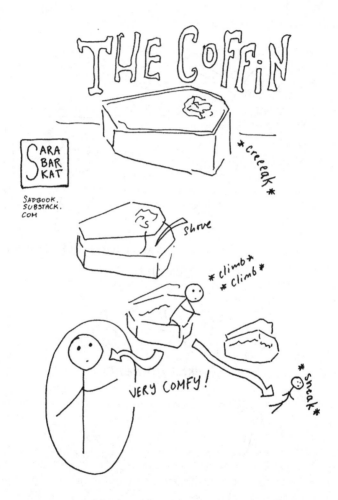

NO·APOLOGY SWEETS

SARA
BAR
KAT

SOMEBODY PUT THIS BAG ON
THE DOOR... IT IS FULL OF
NO-APOLOGY SWEETS.

THEY ARE
VERY
YUMMY...

HOWEVER

NOT AS YUMMY AS THEY COULD BE.

WHEN THEY COME WITHOUT
AN APOLOGY (AND BECAUSE
THE PERSON WHO PUT THEM
THERE KEEPS DOING THE
SAME THING OVER AND OVER)

WELL...

SOMEONE
THOUGHT
I NEEDED
NO-APOLOGY
SWEETS.

[BECAUSE THEY ARE HERE]

BUT I AM STILL
WAITING

I WILL EAT
THEM ALL...

FOR THE
PERSON
TO CHANGE.

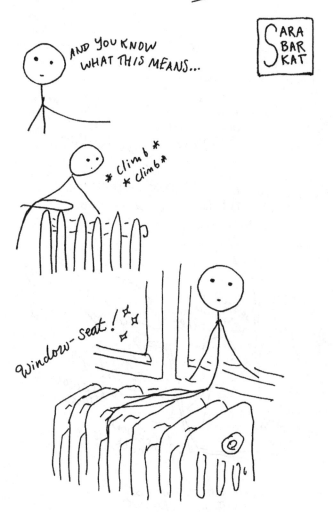

HEADLESS

THE NIGHTMARE

THIS SADBOOK CAME TO ME IN A DREAM

LEAF PAINTING

TODAY I WENT OUTSIDE
AND I PAINTED
A CLAY LEAF.

IT IS VERY DIFFERENT
TO PAINT OUTSIDE!

THE AIR IS CRISP...

AND ONCE,
A REAL
LEAF JOINED ME!

SARA BARKAT

SCRIBBLY

BUSY

SO PREPARED

I THINK I WILL JUST CHECK HOW MANY COMICS I HAVE SCHEDULED...

O ZERO

ZERO...

AH...

ONE MOMENT...

I WILL BE RIGHT BACK...

404

SADBOOK IS NOT AVAILABLE, DRAWING NEW COMICS

A TOY CAR

ZOOM ZOOM ZOOM

weeee!

I WILL OPEN UP THE ENGINE ...

AND GO ON A DRIVE !

THE ARTIST IS SICK

So I WILL BRING
A TISSUE BOX...

A TV SHOW...

A BOWL OF FOOD...

AND A WARM SWEATER...

* pat *
* pat *

AND WE CAN SIT TOGETHER !

SADBOOK ILLUSION

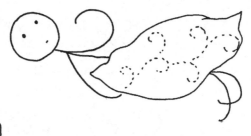

LIMINAL SADBOOK

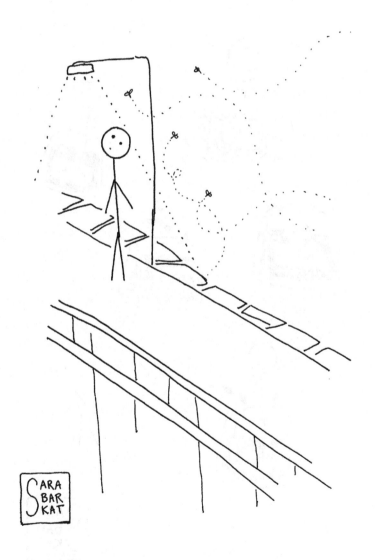

TAKING A DIP

EVERGREEN CONTENT

ON A ROLL!

HOPE

SADBOOK ORIGIN STORY

One day in late December of 2022, the Sadbook artist started doodling. She was intrigued, because somehow this seemed like the beginning of a story—of a stick figure human who might have more to say, more to think, more to do and discover. Here are the eight little pictures that started it all...

electrical impulses
only some
Still living

Memories

ALONE.

No mouth

FOLLOW THE ONGOING STORY

Join the Artist, little Sadbook human, and a
dedicated community of Sadbook readers at ...

sadbook.substack.com

Do you see something in this collection
that you'd like to order as a print? Just ask the Artist
to add it to the Sadbook shop!

Ask on Instagram at
instagram.com/sadbookcollections

or on Substack at
sadbook.substack.com

Made in the USA
Middletown, DE
01 February 2024

48919192R00146